D1356850

YOU ARE
EATING
PLASTIC
EVERY DAY

What's in Our Food?

by Danielle Smith-Llera

Consultant:
Michael Wert, PhD, Marquette University, USA

raintree
a Capstone company — publishers for children

Raintree is an imprint of Capstone Global Library Limited, a company incorporated in England and Wales having its registered office at 264 Banbury Road, Oxford, OX2 7DY – Registered company number: 6695582

www.raintree.co.uk
myorders@raintree.co.uk
Text © Capstone Global Library Limited 2020
The moral rights of the proprietor have been asserted.

Edited by Michelle Bisson
Designed by Sarah Bennett
Original illustrations © Capstone Global Library Limited 2020
Picture research by Kelly Garvin
Production by Katy LaVigne
Originated by Capstone Global Library Ltd
Printed and bound in India

ISBN 978 1 4747 8898 4 (hardback)
ISBN 978 1 4747 8899 1 (paperback)

British Library Cataloguing in Publication Data
A full catalogue record for this book is available from the British Library.

Acknowledgements
We would like to thank the following for permission to reproduce photographs: Alamy: Hera Vintage Ads, 47, Paulo Oliveira, 31, 25; Capstone Press/Karon Dubke, cover; Newscom: AUGIER/OCEANCLEANUP/SIPA, 39, Everett Collection, 46, Paula de Oliveira/NHPA Avalon, 5, 16 (bottom), Paula de Oliveira/NHPA/Avalon.red, 27, WP#ECAF/Euan Cherry/WENN, 17; Shutterstock: alessandro guerriero, 50 (top), Alexey Slyusarenko, 49, AmySachar, 56, Andrey Yaroslavtsev, 10, DeawSS, 28, Drawii, 26, goldenporshe, 34, Inegvin, 10, irin-k, 11, Ivaschenko Roman, 43, Jirawut, 37, Kamal Jafarov, 10, Kidsada Manchinda, 42, Kopnstantin Faraktinov, 32, KstockPhoto, 35, KYTan, 16 (top), Mark Agnor, 23, Maxim Blinkov, 12, mexrix, 1, Mike Workman, 40, Odua Images, 35, Oleksandr Grechin, 50 (bottom), Pann_Churcherd, 36, petovarga, 53 (bottom), PhilipYb Studio, 53 (top), Pro_Vector, 14, Pyty, 18-19, Rich Carey, 6, Richard Whitcombe, 21, RTimages, 55, Sergei Leto, 57, stockcreations, 54, Supriya07, 15, Tim Evseev, 10, vchal, 8-9, Vectorpocket, 41
Design elements: Shutterstock/iamaimmy

Contents

CHAPTER ONE

PLASTIC
ON THE MOVE

Wild seabirds on Midway Island walk up to visitors, close enough to chew their shoelaces. Out here in the middle of the north Pacific Ocean, these grey and white albatrosses have no predators to fear. So they are not afraid of people, though maybe they should be. Humans are responsible for great suffering on their island. Scientists, photographers and film crews have travelled for thousands of miles to take a closer look at the disturbing evidence.

A small pile of bones and feathers marks each place where an albatross has died. The body decays, but it leaves behind a startlingly colourful collection. Bottle tops, toothbrushes, pens, small toys, cigarette lighters and other plastic waste are found where a bird's stomach once was. How did this happen? Seabirds swoop to the ocean surface to scoop up small fish into their beaks – and floating plastic waste too. Seabirds mistake it for food and feed it to their chicks at home. Plastic is not digestible. It crowds their stomachs, so the birds starve. Scientists have found plastic inside nearly every dead chick on Pacific islands like Midway. More than 90 per cent of seabirds have eaten plastic, scientists believe.

This seabird, found on Midway Island, died from ingesting plastic waste.

Seabirds are not the only animals that are eating these unnatural meals. To a sea turtle, a floating plastic bag looks like a tasty jellyfish. Inside their stomachs, bags trap gas and make the animals too buoyant to dive for food or escape predators. To a sperm whale, rippling plastic looks just like a meal of squid. Scientists discovered that one young whale found in Thailand had died after it ate 80 plastic bags.

To people, floating plastic waste looks ugly and depressing, not tasty. But that does not keep us safe. The same ocean that carries plastic to marine creatures is serving plastic waste back to us in our food and beverages.

Fact

Researchers off Canada's west coast in 2013 found glitter, fake snow and bean bag filler in seawater samples. These human-made materials were part of around 9,200 microplastics they found per cubic metre. This amount is like emptying one salt shaker full of microplastics into about three full bathtubs.

If plastic can't move itself, how does it go anywhere at all?

Plastic's journey is full of surprises. Its path depends on small decisions people make, often without thinking. What happens to a plastic bottle once the water is guzzled? What about the plastic spoon once the ice cream is gone? Or the plastic straw once the milkshake is slurped up? Or plastic bags once the groceries are put away in the fridge? Rubbish bins are often nearby. Finding a recycling bin might require a hunt. Each bin will take plastic on a very different trip.

Let's follow the recycling path first. Into a recycling bin goes the plastic. A truck hauls it away to a sorting facility. Sensors use X-rays or infrared light to separate plastics made of different chemicals. Sorted plastics are then hauled to a recycling facility. They are washed, ground into flakes, melted together, squeezed out like toothpaste and snipped into pieces. These pellets are shipped to manufacturing plants where they can take familiar shapes again. Straws are squeezed out in tubes of polystyrene. This plastic is denser than water and keeps a straw from floating up in a drink. This plastic is also rigid enough to be moulded into plastic cutlery. Air blows a light but strong plastic called polyethylene into thin grocery bags or sturdy water bottles.

How can recycling keep up? The world is now producing more than 300 million tonnes of plastic each year. Only about 9 per cent of plastic waste is recycled. For decades, the USA and the UK have exported much of their recyclable materials to other countries, mostly Asia.

Much of it is not recycled because it is too dirty or not the right kind of plastic. Some is burned or re-exported to other countries. Eventually, unwanted plastic lands in overflowing landfills. Ever-growing mountains of rubbish rise in large Asian cities such as Manila in the Philippines and Jakarta in Indonesia. They do not have the technology to manage the rubbish of millions of residents. And for some of the plastics that end up there, their journeys have just begun.

Now let's follow the path of plastic tossed into rubbish bins. It joins left-over food and other things people throw away rather than reusing or recycling. The average person

in the UK throws away their own body weight in rubbish every 7 weeks. Trucks will haul some of the rubbish away to dump at landfills. At the landfill, some of it is burned. Bulldozers heap the rest onto hills. Thick plastic liners block the waste's toxic liquids and gases from seeping into surrounding soil and air. When there is no more room, the rubbish pile is covered with deep soil and planted with trees. The landfill's only job is to store waste. Plastic buried in a landfill can remain unchanged for up to 1,000 years.

A day without plastic

"No one cares about our planet except us," Hannah Testa remembers saying as a four-year-old child, leaving a shop with her mum. The young American had noticed that her mother was the only shopper with reusable bags. In 2017, 14-year-old Testa stood at a microphone to persuade politicians in her state of Georgia to help spread the news of plastic pollution. That's why senators there voted to make February 15 "Plastic Pollution Awareness Day". Each year, residents and businesses challenge themselves to give up disposable plastic straws, bottles and bags for one day. Testa believes it can become a year-round habit. "I hope some day, we will look back and say: 'Can you believe we used to use plastic straws?'"

She tells young audiences around the world, "There is no doubt that you too can do what I have done." Testa helps create materials for teachers to educate young people about the health of the ocean – and to create activists. Testa tells listeners, "If we children join together and use the power of our collective voices, we can force change!"

But not all plastic that is thrown away ends up in rubbish bins. People carelessly throw plastics into waterways – often illegally. Even nature itself can cause water pollution. Rainwater can cause overflows in rubbish dumps. It carries this waste into storm sewers and onwards to rivers, lakes and oceans. Researchers estimate up to 2.4 million tonnes of plastic travels down rivers into the ocean every year. That's comparable to a bin lorry emptying a load of plastic into the ocean every minute.

WHAT HAPPENS TO PLASTIC BOTTLES WHEN WE'RE FINISHED WITH THEM?

Don't recycle
Two-thirds of plastic bottles are not recycled.

Recycle
One-third of plastic bottles are recycled.

Landfill
Collected with other rubbish, bottles are dumped into landfills.

Collection
Collected with other recyclables, bottles are deposited at sorting facilities.

Decomposition
A plastic bottle takes about 450 years to decompose.

Separation
Plastic bottles are separated from other materials.

Sale
Bottles are squashed, baled into cubes and sold to reprocessing plants.

Reprocessing
Bottles are sorted into different plastics, chopped into flakes, washed and decontaminated.

Product manufacture
Recycled plastics are used to make new bottles and other plastic products.

Drifting plastic waste can land on shore, joining other litter pushed up by waves. Still, scientists were shocked by a discovery on a South Pacific island in 2017. The closest inhabited places were thousands of miles away. Yet scientists found that the beaches of Henderson Island were cluttered with bottles, loose bottle tops, yogurt pots, fishing nets, broken toys and other waste.

Henderson Island is one of the most plastic-polluted places in the world – even though no one lives there. Plastic waste is well equipped for long voyages. This sturdy material can last for centuries. But plastic does not roam ocean currents without direction. It travels along predictable paths. A lost cargo of bath toys proved that.

Why is far-away plastic waste my problem?

A load of newly manufactured yellow plastic ducks tumbled off a container ship in 1992. Thousands were launched into Pacific Ocean currents. Over the next decade, toys landed on the shores of South America, Europe, Australia and even the Arctic. Oceanographer Curtis Ebbesmeyer recognized a pattern. Currents in each ocean circulate water like a giant toilet. Water at the edges picks up anything floating and draws it to the centre. These thousand-mile whirlpools are called gyres.

The gyre coughs up its load of plastic onto any island or shore in its way. Beaches catch an astonishing amount of this gyre-driven plastic. Of all the rubbish on Henderson

Island beaches, an estimated 99.8 per cent is plastic. This plastic has travelled a long way. Information printed on products sold in Hawaii, USA is usually printed in English. But containers washing up on Pacific Island beaches are also printed in Russian, Chinese, Indonesian and Vietnamese. Gyre motion explains how plastic got there. It also explains the next stage of plastic's journey: its stealthy path into our stomachs.

Fact

A microscopic fibre can help police connect a suspect to a crime. Researchers have used the same technology to identify plastics that are to blame for releasing microplastics. A beam of infrared light scans microfibres caught inside clams and oysters and matches them to a database of types of plastic textiles manufactured around the world.

Plastic waste can travel across ocean waters and arrive in different continents. Coastlines are littered with waste.

CHAPTER TWO

TINY
HAZARDS

Sailboat captain Charles Moore has navigated fierce winds that have even snapped his mast. Yet, while crossing the North Pacific Ocean in 1997, he experienced something that scared him far more. Plastic buoys, crates and knotted nets floated past his boat. Growing up in California, on the west coast of the United States, he was familiar with plastic waste floating near city docks. Moore also saw it scattered on beaches where he surfed. But this plastic was hundreds of miles from land. He then saw something new. Beneath the ocean surface, Moore spotted tiny plastic flakes fluttering around. He saw them for days as his sailboat crossed the centre of the gyre. They reminded him of spices sprinkled in a great salty soup.

Moore reached shore and spread the news about these bits, or microplastics, at sea. Headlines called what he had

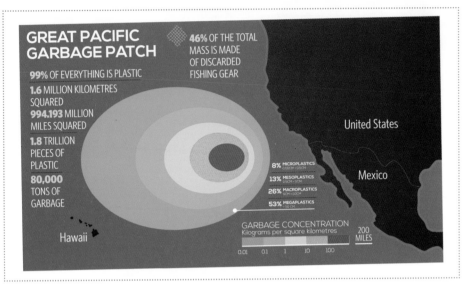

GREAT PACIFIC GARBAGE PATCH

99% OF EVERYTHING IS PLASTIC

1.6 MILLION KILOMETRES SQUARED
994.193 MILLION MILES SQUARED
1.8 TRILLION PIECES OF PLASTIC
80,000 TONS OF GARBAGE

46% OF THE TOTAL MASS IS MADE OF DISCARDED FISHING GEAR

United States

Mexico

Hawaii

8% MICROPLASTICS
13% MESOPLASTICS
26% MACROPLASTICS
53% MEGAPLASTICS

GARBAGE CONCENTRATION
Kilograms per square kilometres

200 MILES

0.01   0.1   1   10   100

There are 80,000 tonnes of garbage in the Great Pacific Garbage Patch alone – and it's one of five such patches worldwide.

seen the "Great Northern Pacific Garbage Patch". People at first thought it was an island of rubbish. They imagined it was solid enough to walk on. But the microplastics problem is far more disturbing.

Moore headed back to the North Pacific gyre to study the plastic problem. His crew dragged nets along the ocean's surface. First they captured plastic drinks bottles, yogurt containers, umbrella handles, toothbrushes and footballs. It was no surprise to find that most of this floating waste was plastic. It makes up an estimated 90 per cent of all rubbish.

But Moore's fine-meshed nets skimmed up some alarming samples. He found familiar jelly-like clumps of microscopic organisms called plankton. But unnaturally colourful plastic confetti was mixed into every single sample. He headed back home with jars full of the plastic-flecked seawater. He needed to show people what was happening to the ocean.

Who is dumping these microplastics into the ocean?

Beans, vegetables and meat chunks soften and break apart after hours simmering in a soup. Plastics in the ocean do too. But the process takes more than hours of heat on a cooker. It requires years of the sun's ultraviolet rays. This intense, invisible light damages skin and causes sunburn. It bleaches colours in signs, car paint and objects left outside for a long time. It turns floating plastic pale and brittle.

Breaking plastic into pieces takes stirring, like soup. Ocean currents do that work, but very slowly. It takes about a decade for a water bottle to float from California to Japan and back again. Ocean currents move through five major gyres. Plastics can and do ride across the globe – across the Pacific, Atlantic and Indian Oceans – as if on a giant conveyor belt. Decades of sunlight and thousands of miles of jostling water gradually shred it to bits. These gyre-shredded microplastics are the size of a grain of rice or smaller.

THE FIVE MAJOR GYRES

1 North Pacific Gyre

5 North Atlantic Gyre

Indian Ocean Gyre

3 South Pacific Gyre

4 South Atlantic Gyre

2

Popular skin cleansers contain thousands of microbeads. They are flushed down our drains only to be eaten by seabirds and fish.

Some plastics in the gyre need no shredding at all. Factories have already done the work. Plastic microbeads give some toothpastes and soaps a rough texture for scrubbing. Biodegradable materials, such as ground-up apricot seeds, can do the same job. But plastic microbeads are less expensive to use. And manufacturers need a lot of them. Just one bottle of face scrub can hold more than 300,000 plastic microbeads. After they are used for polishing teeth and cleaning faces, tap water washes microbeads down bathroom drains. They begin a journey through sewer pipes that can end in the sea.

Mermaids' tears

They are lentil-sized and lentil-shaped, but they are not food. Waves push countless microplastics onto beaches, from the UK to South Africa and Hong Kong. These "nurdles" are factory-made plastic pellets. This raw plastic is ready for dyes, additives and heat to turn them into plastic products. These nurdles travel to factories by the billions. But there are accidents. Nurdles escape into drains and waterways during sorting, loading and unloading. They join nurdles already floating in the sea from containers that fall off ships and split open.

Activists call nurdles "mermaids' tears" for a sad reason. To fish and seabirds, bite-sized plastics look like food. Researchers found plastic in the stomachs of 95 per cent of dead birds in a North Sea study. They found 273 nurdles in one bird alone. Businesses making or transporting nurdles should clean up spills, activists say. But for now the enormous job belongs to volunteers of all ages. In only two hours, one clean-up team on a UK beach collected 450,000 nurdles.

Most of the ocean-travelling microplastics are even smaller. Polyethylene, the same plastic as in water bottles, can be spun into fine threads invisible to the naked eye. These microfibres are shorter than the width of a pencil tip and thinner than a human hair. They make lightweight clothing that keeps people dry, warm or cool. Natural fibres like wool or cotton cannot do it better. What's more, it is less expensive to make clothing from plastic microfibres than natural fibres.

Unfortunately, plastic-spun clothing also becomes plastic waste. It is cheap to replace as fashions change. It is estimated that £140 million worth of clothing in the UK

POLLUTION: FROM RIVERS TO OCEAN

Rivers

1. Niger
2. Nile
3. Indus
4. Ganges
5. Mekong
6. Yangtze
7. Yellow
8. Pearl
9. Hai He
10. Amur

Fact

Ten rivers deliver more than 90 per cent of the ocean's plastic waste. The Yangtze River in China carries the most, with 1.5 million tonnes of plastic a year. That list includes the Nile River in Egypt, the Ganges River in India and the Niger River in West Africa.

goes into landfill each year. Much of this clothi~
of plastic.

Plastic-based clothing causes trouble even w
don't throw it away. The fierce churning of a washing
machine loosens microfibres. Each wash can loosen
700,000 microfibres in one load of laundry. One thick
fleece jacket can shed 100,000 fibres per wash. These
microfibres drain away with water into sewer pipes at an
alarming rate. About 30,000 kilograms (64,000 pounds) of
microfibres are released into US water systems every day.
Researchers believe that 40 per cent of them escape into
the ocean. How do they know? Almost every ocean water
sample they collect contains microfibres.

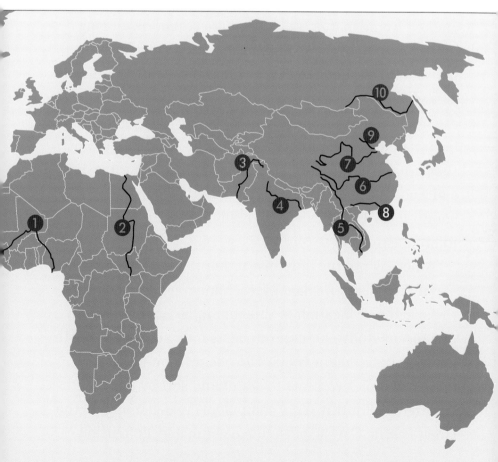

Whether made by factories or gyres, microplastics are everywhere. They make up an estimated 85 per cent of plastics polluting the world's beaches.

Aren't tiny plastic pieces better than ugly piles of plastic waste?

An unwanted cardboard box in water can break apart completely in weeks, leaving no trace of cardboard behind. Even though plastic is made from petroleum – a nature-made liquid created in the earth from ancient living matter – it is far more stubborn. During plastic manufacturing, high heat and chemicals shuffle petroleum's carbon molecules into new, tightly connected arrangements. These interlocking chains, called polymers, are not found in nature. Organisms like worms and bacteria biodegrade materials like wood and paper. But they are not able to break apart plastic. So microplastics swirl endlessly around the gyre like flakes inside a snow globe. The oceans may hold more than 51 trillion microplastics.

Moore is not the only researcher to worry and wonder about the plastic-flecked gyres. Many people now track the speed and location of this microplastic invasion. In one recent study, 30 research boats rode across the North Pacific gyre dragging nets. The one million plastics collected took two years to count and sort by hand with tweezers. With this data, computers created a map of the Great Pacific Garbage Patch. An estimated 1.8 trillion pieces of plastic float in an area about three times the size of France. That's 250 pieces of plastic for every person on Earth.

But scientists are not satisfied with these guesses. Nets can only trap plastics near the ocean's surface. Scientists believe that only 1 per cent of plastic pollution in the ocean has been identified. The rest could be below the surface. Microscopic plants floating at the ocean's surface attach to microplastics. They soak up sunlight to make food. They can also force microplastics to sink – even 11,000 metres (36,000 feet) down into the ocean's deepest trench. But there is an even better hiding place for microplastics: inside living bodies.

Fact

Each year, fishing nets catch more than 100 million tonnes of fish that feed billions of people. Before the invention of plastic, the nets were made of cotton, hemp and other natural fibres. Today, lost plastic fishing nets make up nearly half of all the ocean's plastic pollution.

CHAPTER THREE

EAT UP

A fly lands on your chips. Hundreds of bacteria that could make a person ill might be hitching rides on its legs and body. But there are also invisible ways for dangers to sneak into your food. That's why the British government works hard to make sure your food is safe to eat.

School canteens, grocery stores, restaurants, vending machines and any business serving food must follow strict rules. Anyone preparing food must cook and refrigerate the food they serve at certain temperatures to keep bacteria from growing. Raw foods must not touch cooked foods. Before adding any chemicals to keep food fresh or change its colour, taste or texture, food companies must prove that the chemicals are safe to eat. Water from the tap or in bottles is regularly checked for toxic minerals and bacteria. Experts also check for poisonous pesticides that have washed into waterways.

Consumers must know what goes into their mouths. Labels on packaged food must list all ingredients. Still, dangerous ingredients can still sneak in. Bacteria can cling to vegetables grown in contaminated earth. Restaurant or supermarket employees with unwashed hands can also pass bacteria to food. When illness carried by food sickens or even kills people, the government steps in with a plan to keep the infection from spreading further.

People packaging raw meat keep their hands covered to avoid passing on bacteria. Ironically, the gloves they wear are plastic.

Food safety officials are expected to look for early warning signs of a food-borne emergency. But it is not clear how the government can protect people from consuming plastic in their food. Experts are not even sure how harmful it is. Is it really safe to eat a tuna fish sandwich or a basket of scampi? Is it even safe to sprinkle sea salt over a meal? Many people are paying attention to warning signs.

Not only activists like Moore, scientists and government officials – but young consumers too.

Why can't I see plastic waste in my food?

Captain Moore proudly hooked a 45-kilo (100-pound) tuna inside the North Pacific gyre in 1997. The enormous fish was large enough to feed his crew all the way home to California. He had seen microplastics at sea on that history-making trip. But he didn't know he was probably eating microplastics in each mouthful of tuna. How can deep-diving tuna ever cross paths with floating plastic?

Many hungry animals depend on plants for food. Many also depend on each other. On land, sunlight feeds plants. These plants are food for insects and rodents. Predators such as hawks and foxes eat these rodents. In the ocean, sunlight feeds microscopic plants called phytoplankton floating near the ocean's surface. Tiny herbivores called zooplankton feast on this microscopic salad. Meanwhile, small fish such as sardines depend on plankton for their own meals. As on land, animals eat but are also eaten. Small fish become meals for larger fish such as Moore's tuna.

That's how life in the ocean works when nature is in charge. But what happens now that microplastics float among plankton? A microscope aimed at a seawater sample captured a strange sight in 2015: plankton swallowing

A fish larva
eats microplastics.
These small pieces of plastic
in the oceans are created mainly
from the breakdown of bigger plastics.

floating microbeads. Another scientist later glimpsed a worm-shaped plankton with a microfibre tangled inside its transparent body. Plastic-stuffed stomachs and intestines mean little to no room for nutritious food, whether the consumer is a plankton or a whale.

Plankton are not the only marine animals to be tricked by microplastics. As many as 700 species of marine animals have eaten them, a 2017 study found. To fish, colourful fluttering microplastics can look, and even smell, like food. Researchers in Hong Kong discovered 80 plastic pieces inside just one fish.

Plastic sneaks into our bodies too. In 2018 researchers discovered microplastics in human faeces (poo). The ocean food chain offers an explanation for how it got there. When zooplankton or small fish eat microplastics, the plastics travel up the food chain. People enjoy eating prawns, oysters, crabs and predators such as tuna and salmon.

That puts people at the top of the ocean's food chain. In a 2015 study, researchers bought fish at seafood markets on either side of the Pacific Ocean. They found that one-quarter contained plastics.

Some have called this the ocean's revenge: mincing up plastic waste to feed back to us.

THE PATH OF PLASTIC IN THE FOOD CHAIN

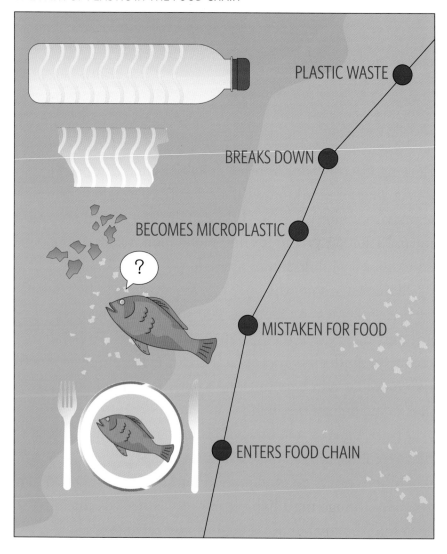

Why could microplastics in food be so dangerous anyway?

Moore's gyre-caught tuna provided his grateful crew with protein-rich meals. In fact, more than 2.5 billion people on Earth depend on seafood for protein. Blood, bone, muscle and brain cells are all made of protein. Proteins also send instructions to cells around the body and fight infection. Now scientists wonder if a sprinkling of plastic in seafood meals could be harming humans.

Added chemicals help plastics take endless useful forms. The government has begun to ban some of these chemicals in plastic toys and food packaging. But plastics sold before these bans are already floating in the ocean.

Dyes change the colour of plastic. Other chemicals make it resistant to ultraviolet light, water or fire. To make plastic containers rigid to hold food or drink, plastic manufacturers have added bisphenol A (BPA). To make plastic flexible for plastic wrap and other food packaging, manufacturers have added phthalates. Plastic made with BPA has also been used to line aluminium cans. These chemical-laden plastics were not designed to enter the body. But the tiny shape and buoyancy of microplastics allow them to do just that.

Scientists have ideas about how these chemicals could affect our health. The body may confuse these human-made chemicals for natural chemicals called hormones. Hormones are messengers, telling the body how to grow and develop. They also trigger emotions and feelings of hunger. Plastic-borne chemicals could interrupt these messages and change the way a body behaves. They might cause life-threatening conditions like high blood pressure. A major concern is the effect of plastics on the brain. Plastics could also affect some of the glands of foetuses, babies and children. Many companies advertise that their products are now BPA-free and phthalate-free. But studies suggest that new plastics replacing them are unhealthy too.

Fact
Cooks living near plastic-littered beaches have found that petroleum-rich plastic waste can quickly light a fire. But breathing its chemical-filled smoke can cause cancer. Designs are improving for stoves that burn plastic safely - and even charge mobile phones at the same time.

There are other dangerous chemicals that manufacturers never added to plastic. Nature has done that work. Rain washes other chemicals from land into the ocean. There they cling to microplastics like swimmers to rafts. Created in labs, these chemicals were originally designed to help people. The chemical DDT was developed in the late 1800s as an insecticide. It was designed to kill disease-carrying mosquitoes and insects that destroy crops. Beginning in the 1920s, polychlorinated biphenyls (PCBs) were added to TVs, refrigerators and industrial equipment. PCBs helped them resist high temperatures. In 1981, the government banned these chemicals in the UK because of growing concerns that they caused cancer. But decades' worth of DDT and PCBs still float in the ocean. They can coat microplastics like a toxic sauce.

PCBs have been found in living bodies – even in organisms living thousands of feet below the Pacific Ocean's surface. They have also been detected in the blood and urine of most people tested. Humans are the most successful predators on Earth. They eat this collection of chemicals stored in the bodies of animals below them in the food chain. This process is called bioaccumulation.

Scientists warn that these plastic-borne chemicals could threaten human health. But they cannot prove it. It is not safe to experiment on humans, so they gather facts and make guesses. Some scientists believe that these chemicals may not reach levels high enough to hurt our bodies – yet. Others see plenty of reasons to panic. Bioaccumulation is a slow but steady process. Microplastics can break down into even smaller pieces called nanoplastics. They measure less than 100 billionths of a metre – small enough to enter the cells of tissues and organs in living organisms.

So if I don't eat seafood,
I can avoid all this trouble?

People could be eating almost 70,000 microplastics a year, even if their meals do not include seafood. Most of these are microfibres. In three years, people could be eating the equivalent of 6.5 cm² of microfibre fabric.

Microplastics seem able to travel up food chains on land. Their journey starts with mosquitoes. When they hatch in water, the caterpillar-like larvae eat microscopic organisms and plants, and microplastics too. Some plastic stays in their bodies even after they develop into winged adult mosquitoes. Birds, bats and other insects feed on mosquitoes and give microplastics the next lift up in land food chains.

Even vegetarian meals may not be safe. When waste water is purified at water treatment plants, a sludge accumulates. It is rich in minerals – but also in waterborne microfibres.

Farmers use it as fertilizer in fields to help crops grow. Scientists are not sure if this contaminated soil is unhealthy for growing our food. But it gives them yet one more source of microplastics to worry about.

It may not matter if our food is healthy if we sprinkle salt on it, or cook with it. Ocean water is sometimes evaporated to produce table salt. As much as 90 per cent of table salt contains microplastics, a 2018 study found. Salt tested in Indonesia was the most plastic-laden salt of all. Indonesia suffers from some of the greatest plastic pollution in the world. You can avoid seafood, but you can't avoid salt. Bodies depend on it to function properly.

Tiny fragments of microplastics (seen in orange) make their way into table salt.

There is yet another stealthy way microplastics slip into our food. Not all microplastics settle into the sludge at water treatment plants. Microfibres were found in 94 per cent of tap water tested in the USA in a 2017 study. Water is an important ingredient in pasta, beans, soup, bread and many other foods. Toxic chemicals riding aboard microplastics add secret ingredients to mixing bowls and cooking pots. Bottled water is not plastic-free either – especially when bottled in plastic. In a world study of 11 brands of bottled water, 93 per cent of water samples contained microplastics. In one popular brand, as many as 10,000 microplastics were found in each litre-sized bottle.

Plastic even floats through the air inside homes. Microfibres in furniture and carpets loosen and float away, joining other dust particles. In one experiment, researchers placed sticky tape next to plates of food. After a 20-minute meal, they examined dust trapped by the tape. It contained more than 100 plastic microfibres. No matter what microplastics are already hiding inside food, an extra dusting of plastic is the topping.

Fast food fears

Young children happily snatch up the plastic toy that arrives with a fast food meal. The British government has banned these plastic additives in some children's products. But the meal may not be phthalate-free. These chemicals can make their way into young people's bodies one mouthful at a time.

Pizza, pasta and burritos, for example, are created in factories. Phthalates can leak in while food passes through plastic tubes and over factory conveyor belts. Many fast food workers even handle fast food with plastic gloves. These plastics only touch food briefly. But experts worry that they can still contaminate food with dangerous chemicals.

Scientists have found that people who eat fast food have up to 40 per cent more phthalates in their bodies than people who do not. The scientists are not sure if fast foods are to blame for the higher phthalate levels. After all, they could not measure phthalate levels in the food. But they used their results to issue a firm warning: avoid restaurants that serve processed, factory-made foods. To be safe, choose restaurants that offer fresh foods that require little contact with plastic before heading to our stomachs.

CHAPTER FOUR

PLASTIC
BE GONE

Restaurants and supermarkets offer many food choices to hungry customers. Ocean water offers many kinds of microplastics to hungry organisms too. Ocean water samples reveal that the most popular options are polyethylene terephthalate (PET) and polypropylene (PP). That means that plastics in water bottles, food packaging and shopping bags are the most frequent travellers through our digestive systems. The proof is in the toilet. Researchers found these microplastics in the faeces of the participants in a 2018 study.

It is no surprise that food is flecked with bits of plastic bags and bottles. The UK's top 10 supermarkets produce over 1.1 billion single-use bags, 958 million "bags for life" and 1.2 billion plastic fruit and vegetable bags every year.

If everyone sent plastic waste to recycling centres, would there still be a problem?

Recycling centres are picky. In fact, recycling bins can be gateways to landfills for some plastics. Plastic might get rejected if it is too dirty or mixed up carelessly with non-plastic waste. Rejected plastic waste might be tangled up with non-recyclable plastic such as fairy lights, hoses, clothes hangers and waterproof shoes. Recycling centres look for plastics with labels that identify the type. Plastic without labels – bin bags, Ziploc bags, bubble wrap, crisp

Material to be recycled is moved along a conveyor belt
to the next step in the sorting process.

packets, sweet wrappers and so much more —cannot be recycled. Too little useful material remains after the process of recycling.

Recycling plastic is expensive and a lot of work. Running a recycling centre 24 hours a day requires water, energy, people and equipment, including conveyor belts, sorters and crushers. Burying plastic in landfills can cost less. When the price of petrol falls, manufacturing new plastic can cost less than recycling used plastic. Businesses save money, but plastic waste continues to pile up.

For more than 25 years, the UK and other European nations, the USA, Canada and Japan have passed the plastic problem on to other countries. They have even made a profit selling their plastic waste. Countries – mostly in Asia – buy used plastic to recycle

PLASTIC RECYCLING CODES

1
PETE
Polyethylene Terephthalate
fizzy drinks • water bottles • shampoo bottles • mouthwash bottles • peanut butter jars

2
HDPE
High Density Polyethylene
milk, water, juice jugs • detergent bottles • yogurt pots • margarine tubs • shopping bags

3
V
Vinyl
clear food packaging • shampoo bottles

4
LDPE
Low Density Polyethylene
bread bags • frozen food bags • squeezable bottles (mustard, honey)

5
PP
Polypropylene
ketchup • yogurt pots • margarine tubs

6
PS
Polystyrene
most toys • egg cartons • cups and plates

7
OTHER
ketchup bottles • large water bottles • some juice bottles

into much-needed raw plastic for their own manufacturing. China bought two thirds of the world's plastic waste in 2016. But in 2018 the country decided to strictly limit the plastics it would buy. Plastic waste soon began piling high inside warehouses around the world. Many countries scrambled to find other places to send it. City officials and waste managers in some US states even began giving residents new instructions: throw recyclable materials into rubbish bins.

Can't scientists find new ways to get rid of this plastic waste?

Nature is a skilful recycler. A dead organism makes a healthy meal for microscopic organisms like bacteria. These decomposers break down the bodies of even the largest predators into nutrients that living organisms can use.

What a surprise for scientists to discover that some animals actually have an appetite for plastic! In a sample of waste water from a recycling centre, scientists discovered bacteria at work on plastic water bottles. The bacteria can break down the thick plastic in weeks. Scientists also discovered that a type of caterpillar called a waxworm has an appetite for plastic. Normally it munches on beehive wax, but its saliva can also break apart the tightly bound polymers in the synthetic material. Holes appear in a shopping bag full of waxworms in just hours. These organisms could help landfills biodegrade plastics instead of simply stashing them out of sight. But this solution could also be risky. Breeding waxworms for this enormous job would put beehives in greater danger if waxworms ventured beyond landfills. Our food supply depends on bees to pollinate crops.

Plastic can actually be made from food to attract many decomposers. Corn, wheat, sugar cane, mushrooms, orange peels and milk sound like items on a shopping list. But those items have been used to create food-based plastics in labs and shaped into items such as cling film, plastic cutlery and packaging. These bioplastics are already in use today.

But feeding plastic to nature's decomposers is not so simple. Many food-based plastics marked "biodegradable" are only biodegradable in certain environments. To break down, bioplastics need ultraviolet light at the ocean's surface. Yet plastics in the ocean often sink far from sunlight to the dark ocean floor. To break down, bioplastics need high temperatures that only a special recycling centre can provide. Packed inside landfills, bioplastics can last as long as petroleum-based plastics. Inside the mountain of rubbish, bacteria cannot get the oxygen they need to decompose anything very quickly, whether an orange peel, aluminium can or plastic spoon.

So far, no kind of recycling can keep up with the amount of plastic waste produced each year. Some experts predict that by 2050 the ocean's contents will be alarmingly out of balance. If all the fish and all the plastic could be weighed, there would be more plastic.

So not using plastics is the only way to keep it out of our food?

It takes scientists to find a way to stop toxic plastic leaking into our food. It also takes people working to change the way others think about wasting plastic. Many need to get involved to work on a solution. Many small bits of plastic create a plastic invasion. It takes many activists working together to help resist it.

When 16-year-old Boyan Slat of The Netherlands went scuba diving in Greece, the trip turned out to be life-changing. "I saw more plastic bags than fish," he remembered. "Everyone said to me: 'Oh there's nothing you can do about plastic once it gets into the oceans,' and I wondered whether that was true." Two years later, in 2013, he founded "The Ocean Cleanup," an organization of scientists, engineers and technicians working on ways to

Boyan Slat and his team set out with high hopes of cleaning the ocean in 2018. Their effort failed, but they soon went to work on a new solution.

clean up ocean plastic. The organizers had hoped the 600-metre (2,000-foot) tube-shaped buoy, dragging a 3-metre (10-foot) skirt, would capture tonnes of plastic. But by the end of 2018, the £19-million ($25-million) system hadn't collected much plastic. The ocean had even broken it apart. But the Ocean Cleanup team views failure as part of the process of experimentation. "We think the fastest way to clean the ocean is to learn by doing," said Slat. His team is hard at work on a new solution.

Some activists begin their work at an even younger age. In 2013, 12-year-old Melati Wijsen and her 10-year-old sister, Isabel, wanted to do something about the plastic waste choking the towns, roadsides and beaches of their home – Bali, Indonesia. Every day, residents and visitors dump 5,000 tonnes of rubbish directly into the ocean around the island. The sisters decided to tackle the plastic bag problem. Around the world, people use up to 5 trillion of them a year. "Everybody uses plastic bags. People toss them from cars, put them in bins and where do they go? Into rice fields, rivers, the ocean," Wijsen said. With

The beaches of Bali, Indonesia, once a holiday paradise, are now covered with plastic waste.

Fact

Cleaning up trillions of ocean microplastics doesn't sound impossible to everyone. Activists and engineers are working on solar-powered, diving vacuum cleaners. Another option is a system of miles-long plastic pipes that skim up plastics while not disturbing marine life below. A 12 year-old girl from Massachusetts, USA, created an award-winning design for an underwater robot that hunts microplastics with infrared light.

the help of student volunteers, she and her sister clean up beaches. They urge shop owners and shoppers to use reusable bags made from cloth and recycled newspaper. Their "Bye, Bye Plastic Bag" campaign has spread across Asia to the USA and Mexico. "We have a lot of kids spreading the word now," Wijsen said. "It's really cool."

Nine-year-old Milo Cress made a small request at a restaurant in Vermont, USA, in 2010. He noticed that drinks were always served with straws. A straw contains very little plastic. But after some research, Cress estimated that people in the US could be using as many as 500 million drinking straws a day. Wind and water easily carry off this plastic, which is light as a feather. He asked the restaurant owner to only give out straws to customers who asked for them. "It saved them money, it would be good for the environment, and there wouldn't be so much waste," he explained later. "I was worried adults wouldn't listen to me  because I was a kid . . . but I found the opposite to be true." Today his "Be Straw Free" campaign is a large organization that works with schools, businesses and environmental groups. It estimates that today more than half of customers choose to avoid drinking straws if given a choice.

University student Amira Odeh knew why her school in Puerto Rico did not fix broken water fountains: students only drank out of single-use plastic water bottles they bought at the canteen. And, of course, the canteen profited. Odeh's classmates were not unlike many on-the-go students around the world. Every minute of the day, people purchase about one million plastic bottles worldwide. For four years, Odeh worked on a campaign called "No Mas Botellas" ("No More Bottles"). Finally, the university agreed to fix the fountains and started the first ban on plastic water bottles in Latin America. "Back when we started," Odeh said, "no one had reusable bottles. Now I see about half the students carrying one in their backpacks." Students refill these metal bottles at water fountains with signs announcing "Free and Clean Water".

These young activists depend on the help of many others. Nearly 1,000 young people ages 11 to 18 gathered for the 2018 "Ocean Heroes Boot Camp" in New Orleans, USA, to learn from and teach each other how to organize campaigns against plastic pollution. They connected online with young activists meeting in other locations, from Vancouver, Canada, to Nairobi, Kenya.

Seafood plastic?

Tough, translucent prawn shells look a lot like plastic, secondary school student Angelina Arora noticed. Restaurant bins in her hometown of Sydney, Australia, overflow with seafood shells. Could this seafood waste make a substitute for plastics? This serious science student conducted lab experiments for months. At the age of 16, Arora made a discovery. By mixing proteins found in shrimp shells and silk cocoons, she could create a plastic-like material. Strong as shrimp shells and flexible as silk threads, the new material breaks down 1.5 million times faster than petroleum-based plastics. In only 33 days, it biodegrades completely, leaving no dangerous chemical behind.

Arora's invention has won international awards and has attracted the attention of scientists and businesses looking for a safer way to make plastics. "Every time I fail or things don't work out in the lab, I always think back to why I started doing it," she says. "That is to make oceans plastic-free and encourage other young people, especially young girls, to make a difference in the world, in whatever domain their passion lies."

Adult members of environmentalist organizations joined experienced young activists. They shared advice on how to persuade more people to join campaigns. The goal of the annual workshop is "empowering the next generation of ocean health leaders."

A small group of participants put these skills to the test later that year. They had the chance to speak during a meeting of world leaders in Quebec, Canada. "We got them to commit in front of everyone to fight to stop plastic pollution," said 17-year-old participant Carter Ries. His sister, 15-year-old Olivia, said, "We are starting to realize that we need to make a change now. If we don't, then the next generation may not have that chance."

CHAPTER FIVE

PRECIOUS
PLASTIC

It is easy to forget a mouth brace on a lunch tray. Moulded for teeth out of clear plastic, it is nearly invisible and can slide with unwanted food into a canteen bin. But kids and helpful adults will dig through the rubbish to help find this plastic. It's expensive to replace because it is sturdy, mouldable and long-lasting. The qualities that make plastic waste so hard to manage can also make it extraordinarily useful. Mixed into white dental fillings, plastic patches up cavities invisibly. Ground into lenses and set into frames of any colour, plastic sharpens your vision. Puffed into foam soles, plastic cushions your trainers. Squeezed into tubes, plastic coats wires to keep electricity away from you as it flows through your devices. It encases your expensive electronics with shock-absorbing and heat-resistant protection.

It is difficult to imagine a world without plastic. Many everyday items were once time-consuming to make and expensive to buy. Toothbrushes were once fitted with pig bristles. Hair combs were once hand-polished from tortoiseshell. Plastics changed all that.

The first modern plastic made a dramatic entrance in the early 1900s. Customers could not get enough of this new synthetic material developed from petroleum by Belgian-American chemist Leo Baekeland in an explosion-prone lab. Sleek, richly coloured "Bakelite" was advertised as the "material of a thousand uses". It could be

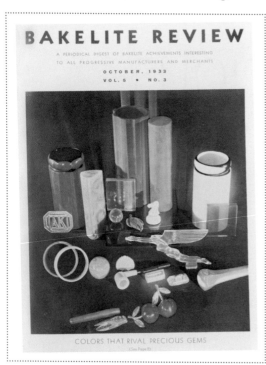

Bakelite was so popular in the 1930s that it had a whole magazine devoted to it.

drilled, moulded and bent into countless forms: doorknobs, steering wheels, radios, telephones, pens, bracelets and even coffins. Chemists set to work inventing more profitable petroleum-based materials.

Plastics helped fight World War II (1939–45). Various kinds of plastics were woven into parachutes and moulded into parts of aeroplanes and guns. Plastics coated antennae and radar cables and cushioned metal helmets. Far more plastic poured out of factories by the end of the war than at the beginning. When the war ended, manufacturers found new customers for mass-produced plastic items: civilians at home.

Plastics promised people an affordable lifestyle. Beginning in the 1950s, plastics began replacing expensive materials such as steel in cars, wood in furniture and glass in food containers. Plastic meant new and modern.

Along with TV dinners, colourful plastic dishware was a staple of the 1950s.

Customers rushed to buy plastic telephones, electrical plugs, squeezy bottles, sticky tape, contact lenses, dolls, building materials, stackable chairs and much more to make daily life easier.

Plastic could save people more than money. It could also save them time. Why wash dirty ceramic plates, glasses, silverware and cloth napkins? Use plastic ones and toss them in the rubbish! This message from advertisements made single-use items part of an exciting new lifestyle. It was called "Throw-Away Living" by a popular magazine.

Canteen lessons

Students in a class at Thomas Starr Middle School in Los Angeles, USA, knew something was wrong in their canteen. They were studying the effects of rubbish on nature but were throwing away plastic foam lunch trays every day. So the classmates raised money to buy themselves bright yellow trays in reusable plastic. Their idea caught the attention of other students. "It was weird at first, but you get used to it," said Martin Gonzalez, a 13-year-old student at the school. "I think some people were actually jealous." The students picked used plastic trays out of the bins and strung 1,260 together. They hung it on a tree in the grounds like a 9-metre (30-foot) snake.

The school district's director of food services took notice. "The students made a statement, we looked at it, and they're right," David Binkle said. In 2012 the entire school district replaced the 40 million disposable plastic trays used every school year with biodegradable paper trays.

Since the 1950s an estimated 5 billion tonnes of plastic have become rubbish. In the 1960s the first plastic waste was spotted floating in the ocean. It was part of a growing collection. And by the 1970s littered roadsides and waterways proved that these plastic items did not disappear when they were thrown away.

No one would dig through waste to find most of this lost plastic. Half of it is designed to be discarded after just one use. A plastic straw, for example, is used for an average of 20 minutes. A plastic bag is useful for an average of 12 minutes and a plastic coffee stirrer for just seconds. About one-third of these single-use plastics end up in the ocean, experts estimate. They join other plastic waste that has been floating there for decades.

Facts

Plastic is doing more than changing our diets - it is helping to change our weather. Sunlight and seawater cause floating plastics to release methane and ethylene. These gases trap Earth's heat. Warmer air and seawater change weather patterns that affect the way crops grow.

Is it time
to ban all plastic?

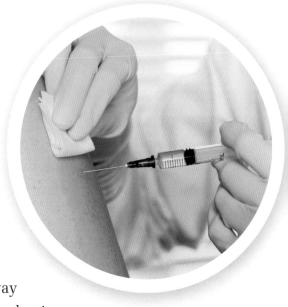

Our lives could be safer without plastics. But it is easy to forget that plastics also make lives safer. In packaging, plastic keeps food fresh, clean and insect-free on the way to our tables. Disposable plastic syringes prevent the spread of disease. Contact lenses, hearing aids, artificial limbs, tubing to unblock veins and life-saving heart valves are all composed of plastic. It also protects lives with seatbelts, car doors filled with plastic foam that is impact-resistant, padded sports helmets and police officers' bulletproof vests. Plastic can save energy and resources. Artificial plastic turf on sports fields does not demand the water and care that real grass does. Plastic insulation means that it takes less energy to keep homes warm or cool. Plastic car parts even help to reduce the dangerous gases released by petroleum burning. They are lighter than metal parts so less fuel is needed to run them.

Plastic improves lives in endless ways. But when plastic becomes useless, it can endanger lives.

So if plastic is dangerous *and* helpful, what do we do with it?

Everyday items become precious when they are scarce. During a solo, round-the-world voyage in 2005, British sailor Ellen MacArthur could not afford to waste any supplies on her sailing boat. She appreciated every bit of her limited supplies of food, fuel, clothing, toothpaste and toilet paper. A realization struck her at sea: people might have a different attitude towards rubbish if they remembered that Earth's resources are limited too.

Throwing away plastic is a waste of energy – especially since Earth's petroleum supplies are limited. Most petroleum is burned up as fuel to run cars and equipment, and to heat buildings. Plastic itself can also produce heat and electricity. All the plastic in US landfills could produce the same energy as an estimated 21 billion litres of gasoline – enough to power 8.9 million cars for a year. But this solution is not risk-free. Burning petroleum-based plastics releases gases, as do petroleum-burning vehicles. This air pollution traps heat that is causing Earth's temperature to rise dangerously.

Fact

Nature can actually make propylene, an important ingredient in plastic water bottles. A spacecraft passing Saturn in 2016 detected the chemical on its moon, Titan. Sunlight breaks down and rearranges chemicals in Titan's air to make chains of carbons like the petroleum-based polymers on Earth.

If single-use plastic can be used long term, it can stay out of the ocean. Businesses both large and small are turning single-use plastic waste into profitable items. Single-use plastics make up an estimated 89 per cent of the ocean's plastic waste. Shoe company Adidas estimated that, in 2018, it saved 36 tonnes of plastic from the ocean. The company's fast-drying and lightweight running shoes are made from 11 plastic water bottles each. Smaller companies are making a difference too. Clothing company ADAY designed the "Waste Nothing Jacket", made from 41 bottles. Another company, Girlfriend Collective, designed leggings made from 25 water bottles. A line of its workout gear is made from recycled plastic fishing nets. Recycled plastic has become a fashion statement as customers eagerly buy up these plastic-spun items. It's a start, but even these clothes will eventually end up in the bin because plastics can usually only be recycled once.

Building out of plastic gives it a long-term home. Half the supply of steel, another human-made material, goes into construction and stays useful for decades, while half of plastic becomes rubbish in less than a year. Recycled plastic is now helping to build longer-lasting roads. Instead of cracking like asphalt, plastic paving springs back under the weight of passing cars. Bricks made from recycled plastic can build sturdy, affordable homes by locking together like toy building blocks. Park benches, playground equipment, carpets, football strips and even jewellery gives used single-use plastic new value.

These businesses remind people to give used plastic a chance to stay useful – and out of the world's food chains. As servers of food, restaurant owners are taking a special interest in the plastic pollution problem. They are proving

CIRCULAR ECONOMY

In a circular economy, material is reused and recycled rather than used and then thrown away.

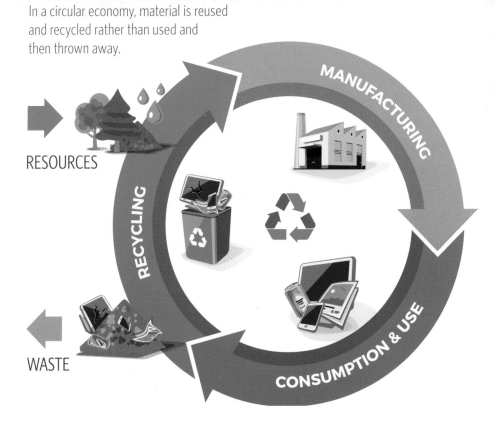

RESOURCES

RECYCLING

MANUFACTURING

CONSUMPTION & USE

WASTE

that people can live without creating much waste, or even any at all. Ellen MacArthur learned this lesson on her boat, but anyone can learn it while visiting one of the zero-waste restaurants popping up across the world. Their mission is to avoid the 45,000 kilograms (100,000 pounds) of waste the average restaurant creates a year. Take-away food is offered in recyclable containers – or not at all. Restaurant diners can eat with washable plates and cutlery at tables sometimes made of colourful recycled plastic. They drink restaurant-filtered tap water served in reusable glass bottles. Vegetables and eggs arrive from nearby farms without plastic packaging. Cooks work longer in the kitchen to prepare fresh ingredients, avoiding prepared foods in plastic-lined cans and plastic packaging.

But what can we do about the decades of plastic already out there? It is in our water, air, soil and food. Scientists and engineers are wrestling with this massive problem. But even young people can learn to slow the flood of plastic waste. One solution is to campaign with local governments to ban certain kinds of plastics, such as straws and shopping bags, as some young people have done.

One young environmental activist decided to live zero-waste while still at university. She now teaches others how to do it. Besides a reusable water bottle, Lauren Singer travels with a set of reusable cutlery and a coffee mug made from lightweight bamboo. She shops with glass containers to fill at shops that sell rice, beans, dry pasta and other dry foods from large bins. She brings fruits and vegetables from farmers' markets to her kitchen in reusable cloth bags. To avoid buying plastic containers, Singer makes her own toothpaste, lotion and deodorant. "It's a series of small choices. Really small, easy little choices that collectively add up to not making any trash," Singer says.

Even living in shop-filled New York City, Singer can fit her rubbish for three years into one 450 gram (16-ounce) glass jar – not much more than the rubbish that MacArthur probably produced during three months at sea. Young people are leading the way towards a new kind of living. "I believe that we need to alter our relationship with plastic," says teenage environmental activist Hannah Testa, "because we aren't going to be able to recycle our way out of this problem."

GET INVOLVED

Millions, billions and trillions. You have heard the plastic pollution problem explained with these enormous numbers. It is easy to feel that you could not possibly make a difference. But each year the Ocean Conservancy proves that people working together can make great changes, one piece of rubbish at a time. For example, on 5 June 2017, volunteers from more than 100 countries headed to beaches to collect rubbish. In just one day, 789,138 people collected 20.5 million pounds of rubbish. Most of it was plastic and headed for ocean gyres and food chains. "If we band together across the world, we can be unstoppable," says activist Hannah Testa. "We just need to care enough to act."

Some things you can do:

- Refuse food packaged in plastic, plastic cutlery and straws. This sends the message to businesses that they will lose customers if they use single-use plastic.

- Take reusable cloth or recycled plastic bags when you shop to avoid using single-use plastic bags.

- Collect any plastic litter you see to help keep it out of the natural environment and, eventually, the ocean.

- Carry a reusable water bottle.

- Set a good example for your friends for how to reuse, refuse or recycle plastic.

SAY NO TO PLASTIC

HELP!

- Start a "Plastic Awareness Day" in your area, like Hannah Testa did. Learn how to get the authorities on your side: hannah4change.org/get-involved/start-your-own-plastic-pollution-awareness-day

- Petition local councillors or politicians to ban certain plastic products, such as shopping bags.

- Join a group of activists to clean up plastic-polluted areas in your area. Or you can organize your own clean-up with friends and post pictures on social media to inspire activists around the world. Example: litterati.org/

- You can find many other suggestions in these links too:
  plasticpollutioncoalition.org/plastic-free-eateries/
  teenvogue.com/story/lauren-singer-zero-waste-lifestyle
  5gyres.org/science-research-hub/
  n-p-i-m.com/html/en/e_fruechte_gemuese_default.htm

GLOSSARY

ban make illegal

bioaccumulation process by which dangerous chemicals accumulate in an organism as they pass up through the food chain

biodegradable capable of being broken down by living organisms

bioplastics useful material created from once-living matter

consumer someone who buys goods for personal use

contaminate make impure or unclean by exposure to pollution

decomposer organisms such as bacteria and fungi that break down dead matter

faeces solid waste released from the bowels of an animal or person

infrared kind of invisible light that can detect objects through temperature

petroleum naturally occurring oil composed of hydrogen and carbon. Petroleum contains substances like gasoline, kerosene and chemicals necessary for making plastics.

polymers substance composed of molecules connected in repeating patterns

synthetic mixture of chemicals that imitates a natural material, like nylon imitates silk

toxic poisonous

ultraviolet kind of invisible light with short waves that can penetrate skin and other surfaces

FIND OUT MORE

Critical thinking questions

Consider what plastic can do, especially with different additives. Make a list of the material's physical qualities. How do these properties make plastic both helpful and harmful to people?

Describe what your daily life would look like without plastic. (Begin with the moment you wake up and end with the moment you go to bed.) Do you think this would be a healthier way of life? Why or why not?

What could be a way to clean microplastics out of our oceans? Use your imagination in addition to what you have learned about the behaviour of microplastics in waterways and the ocean.

Books

No. More. Plastic.: What you can do to make a difference, Martin Dorey (Ebury Press, 2018)

The Incredible Ecosystems of Planet Earth, Rachel Ignotofsky (Wren & Rook, 2019)

Websites

Play the Recycling Game
berecycled.org/game/

What Happens to the Plastic We Throw Out?
nationalgeographic.com/magazine/2018/06/the-journey-of-plastic-around-the-globe/

SOURCE NOTES

p. 9, "No one cares about our planet…" Hannah Testa, "Plastic Pollution Awareness Day Is Headed Your Way," *Earth Guardian*, 2 January 2017, https://www.earthguardians.org/engage/2016/12/28/zke3b23cksnkuewp4fwg2uoatjfsqn Accessed 4 February 2019.

p. 9, "I hope some day, we will look back…" Ann Hardie, "Sunday Conversation with Hannah Testa," *Atlanta Journal Constitution*, 11 June 11 2016, https://www.ajc.com/news/local/sunday-conversation-with-hannah-testa/85QaiufLZImh6qZQ0jQ6aO/ Accessed 4 February 2019.

p. 9, "There is no doubt that you…" Testa, "Plastic Pollution Awareness Day Is Headed Your Way."

p. 9, "If we children join together…" Ibid.

p. 38, "I saw more plastic bags than fish…" Vibeke Venema, "The Dutch boy mopping up a sea of plastic," *BBC News*, 17 October, 2014, https://www.bbc.com/news/magazine-29631332 Accessed 21 January 2019.

p. 40, "Everybody uses plastic bags…" Maryellen McGrath and Morgan Winsor, "'Wonder Girls': How girl-led activists are changing the world," *ABC News*, 6 October 2017, https://abcnews.go.com/International/girls-girl-led-activists-changing-world/story?id=50186933 Accessed 21 January 2019.

p. 41, "We have a lot of kids spreading the word…" Ibid.

p. 41, "It saved them money…" Tanya Basu, "This Kid Single-Handedly Ignited the Plastic Straw Ban Movement," *The Daily Beast*, 24 July 2018, https://www.thedailybeast.com/this-kid-single-handedly-launched-the-plastic-straw-ban-movement Accessed 4 February 2019.

p. 42, "Back when we started…" Natalya Savka, "How Student Activists Are Battling Plastic," *Sierra*, 3 August 2015, https://www.sierraclub.org/sierra/2015-5-september-october/feature/how-student-activists-are-battling-plastic Accessed 4 February 2019.

p. 43, "Every time I fail or things don't…" Lulu Morris, "This Teenage Girl Made a Plastic Bag From Shrimp," *National Geographic*, 20 September, 2018, https://www.nationalgeographic.com/environment/2018/09/angelina-arora-teenager-created-plastic-shrimp-science-fair/ Accessed 4 February 2019.

p. 44, "We got them to commit …" Shaima Shamdeen, "The Boot Camp Trains Young People to Fight Plastic Pollution," *EcoWatch*, 9 July 2018, https://www.ecowatch.com/boot-camp-plastic-pollution-2585161623.html Accessed 4 February 2019.

p. 44, "We are starting to realize that we..." Ibid.

p. 48, "It was weird at first..." Frank Shyong, "L.A. Unified replaces plastic foam cafeteria trays with paper ones," *Los Angeles Times*, 24 August 2012, http://articles.latimes.com/2012/aug/24/local/la-me-plastic-foam-20120824 Accessed 4 February 2019.

p. 48, "The students made a statement..." Ibid.

p. 55, "It's a series of small choices..." Lauren Singer, "How I Fit Three Years' Worth of Trash into One Mason Jar: It's all about the plastic," *Teen Vogue*, 27 May 2015, https://www.teenvogue.com/story/lauren-singer-zero-waste-lifestyle Accessed 4 February 2019.

p. 55, "I believe that we need to alter..." Sybil Bullock, "This Fifteen-Year-Old is Turning the Tide on Plastic Pollution," Greenpeace, https://www.greenpeace.org/usa/stories/fifteen-year-old-turning-tide-plastic-pollution/ Accessed 4 February 2019.

SELECT BIBLIOGRAPHY

Books
Plastic: A Toxic Love Story, Susan Freinkel (Houghton Mifflin Harcourt, 2011).

Plastic Ocean: How a Sea Captain's Chance Discovery Launched a Determined Quest to Save the Oceans, Charles Moore (Avery Publishing, 2011).

Websites and articles
Albeck-Ripka, Livia, "Your Recycling Gets Recycled, Right? Maybe, or Maybe Not," *The New York Times*, 29 May, 2018, https://www.nytimes.com/2018/05/29/climate/recycling-landfills-plastic-papers.html
Accessed 21 January 2019.

Carrington, Damian, "Plastic fibres found in tap water around the world, study reveals," *The Guardian*, 5 September 2017, https://www.theguardian.com/environment/2017/sep/06/plastic-fibres-found-tap-water-around-world-study-reveals Accessed 21 January 2019.

Cernansky, Rachel, "Are synthetic fleece and other types of clothing harming our water?" *The Washington Post*, 30 October 2016, https://www.washingtonpost.com/national/health-science/are-synthetic-fleece-and-other-types-of-clothing-harming-our-water/2016/10/28/eb35f6ac-752e-11e6-be4f-3f42f2e5a49e_story.html?utm_term=.e0e15d-a4f3f9 Accessed 21 January 2019.

Cho, Renee, "The truth about bioplastics," *Phys.org*, 14 December 2017, https://phys.org/news/2017-12-truth-bioplastics.html Accessed 21 January 2019.

Cox, David, "Are we poisoning our children with plastic?" *The Guardian*, 19 February 2018, https://www.theguardian.com/lifeandstyle/2018/feb/19/are-we-poisoning-our-children-with-plastic Accessed 21 January 2019.

Dawson, Claire, "Microfibers: Tiny plastics have a huge impact on our oceans," *The Nature Conservancy*, http://www.washingtonnature.org/fieldnotes/microfibers-tiny-plastics-have-a-huge-impact-on-our-oceans Accessed 21 January 2019.

Evans, Allen, "If you drop plastic in the ocean, where does it end up?" *The Guardian*, 29 July 2017, https://www.theguardian.com/environment/2017/jun/29/if-you-drop-plastic-in-the-ocean-where-does-it-end-up Accessed 21 January 2019.

Georgiu, Aristos, "Microplastics: Every meal you eat may contain more than 100 pieces of plastic, new study finds," *Newsweek*, 4 April 2018, https://www.newsweek.com/microplastics-every-meal-you-eat-may-contain-more-100-pieces-plastic-new-study-872323 Accessed 21 January 2019.

Hunt, Elle, "38 million pieces of plastic waste found on uninhabited South Pacific island," *The Guardian*, 15 May 2017, https://www.theguardian.com/environment/2017/may/15/38-million-pieces-of-plastic-waste-found-on-uninhabited-south-pacific-island Accessed 21 January 2019.

Kaplan, Sarah, "By 2050, there will be more plastic than fish in the world's oceans, study says," *The Washington Post*, 20 January 2016, https://www.washingtonpost.com/news/morning-mix/wp/2016/01/20/by-2050-there-will-be-more-plastic-than-fish-in-the-worlds-oceans-study-says/?utm_term=.cf757e38871e Accessed 21 January 2019.

Meilan, Solly, "Microplastics Found in Human Poop for the First Time," *Smithsonian.com*, 23 October 2018, https://www.smithsonian-mag.com/smart-news/microplastics-found-lurking-human-stool-first-time-180970613/ Accessed 21 January 2019.

Nelson, Bryan, "What can 28,000 rubber duckies lost at sea teach us about our oceans?" *Mother Nature Network*, 1 March 2011, https://www.mnn.com/earth-matters/wilderness-resources/stories/what-can-28000-rubber-duckies-lost-at-sea-teach-us-about Accessed 21 January 2019.

Oksman, Olga, "Fish for dinner? Your seafood might come with a side of plastic," *The Guardian*, 31 August 2016, https://www.theguardian.com/lifeandstyle/2016/aug/31/fish-plastic-pollution-ocean-environment-seafood Accessed 21 January 2019.

"Our planet is drowning in plastic pollution," UN Environment, https://www.unenvironment.org/interactive/beat-plastic-pollution/ Accessed 21 January 2019.

Parker, Laura, "Ocean Life Eats Tons of Plastic – Here's Why That Matters," *National Geographic*, August 16, 2017, https://news.nationalgeographic.com/2017/08/ocean-life-eats-plastic-larvaceans-anchovy-environment/ Accessed 21 January 2019.

Riley, Tess, "The Fight Against the Tiny Plastic Pellets Choking Our Oceans," *Huffington Post*, 11 November 2017, https://www.huffingtonpost.com/entry/oceans-plastics-nurdles-pollution-wildlife_us_5a02def4e4b04e96f0c683c3 Accessed 21 January 2019.

Savka, Natalya, "How Student Activists Are Battling Plastic," *Sierra*, 3 August 2015, https://www.sierraclub.org/sierra/2015-5-september-october/feature/how-student-activists-are-battling-plastic Accessed 21 January 2019.

Storrs, Carina, "Fast food serves up phthalates, too, study suggests," *CNN*, 18 April 2016, https://www.cnn.com/2016/04/15/health/fast-food-phthalates-endocrine-disruptors/index.html Accessed 21 January 2019.

"The Great Pacific Garbage Patch," The Ocean Cleanup, https://www.theoceancleanup.com/great-pacific-garbage-patch/ Accessed 21 January 2019.

Thompson, Andrea, "From Fish to Humans, A Microplastic Invasion May Be Taking a Toll," *Scientific American*, 4 September 2018, https://www.scientificamerican.com/article/from-fish-to-humans-a-microplastic-invasion-may-be-taking-a-toll/ Accessed 21 January 2019.

Watson, Sarah Kiley, "China Has Refused to Recycle the West's Plastics. What Now?" NPR.org, June 28, 2018, https://www.npr.org/sections/goatsandsoda/2018/06/28/623972937/china-has-refused-to-recycle-the-wests-plastics-what-now Accessed 21 January 2019.

"What Is a Circular Economy?" Ellen MacArthur Foundation, https://www.ellenmacarthurfoundation.org/circular-economy/concept Accessed 21 January 2019.

About the author

Danielle Smith-Llera taught children to think and write about literature in the classroom before turning to writing books for them. She grew up collecting shells on beaches in south-eastern Virginia, USA, where a colourful find often turned out to be a plastic fragment. Writing this book made her see them as warnings from the ocean of great danger.

INDEX